HERGÉ

THE ADVENTURES OF TINTIN

THE SECRET
OF
THE UNICORN

EGMONT

The TINTIN books are published in the following languages:

Alsacien	CASTERMAN
English	EGMONT BOOKS LIMITED
	LITTLE, BROWN & Co.
Basque	ELKAR
Bengali	ANANDA
Bernese	EMMENTALER DRUCK
Breton	AN HERE
Catalan	CASTERMAN
Chinese	CASTERMAN/CHINA CHILDREN PUBLISHING
Corsican	CASTERMAN
Danish	CARLSEN
Dutch	CASTERMAN
Esperanto	ESPERANTIX/CASTERMAN
Finnish	OTAVA
French	CASTERMAN
Gallo	RUE DES SCRIBES
Gaumais	CASTERMAN
German	CARLSEN
Greek	CASTERMAN
Hebrew	MIZRAHI
Indonesian	INDIRA
Italian	CASTERMAN
Japanese	FUKUINKAN
Korean	CASTERMAN/SOL
Latin	ELI/CASTERMAN
Luxembourgeois	IMPRIMERIE SAINT-PAUL
Norwegian	EGMONT
Provençal	CASTERMAN
Picard	CASTERMAN
Polish	CASTERMAN/MOTOPOL
Portuguese	CASTERMAN
Romanche	LIGIA ROMONTSCHA
Russian	CASTERMAN
Serbo-Croatian	DECJE NOVINE
Spanish	CASTERMAN
Swedish	CARLSEN
Thai	CASTERMAN
Turkish	YAPI KREDI YAYINLARI
Tibetan	CASTERMAN

Translated by Leslie Lonsdale-Cooper
and Michael Turner

EGMONT
We bring stories to life

Artwork copyright © 1946 by Editions Casterman, Paris and Tournai.
Copyright © renewed 1974 by Casterman.
Text copyright © 1959 by Egmont Books Limited.
First published in Great Britain in 1959 by Methuen Children's Books.
This edition published 2002 by Egmont Books Limited,
239 Kensington High Street, London W8 6SA.

Library of Congress Catalogue Card Numbers Afor 5911 and R 585354
ISBN 1 4052 0622 5

Printed in Spain
5 7 9 10 8 6 4

THE SECRET
OF
THE UNICORN

NEWS IN BRIEF

AN alarming rise in the number of robberies has been reported in the past few weeks. Daring pickpockets are operating in the larger stores, the cinemas and street markets. A well-organised gang is believed to be at work. The police are using their best men to put a stop to this public scandal.

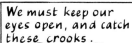

We must keep our eyes open, and catch these crooks.

How about starting in the Old Street Market? Tintin said he was going there this morning. Perhaps we'll meet him.

Good idea. Let's go.

Why, there are Thomson and Thompson.

Hello! ... How are you?

Look who's here!

Tintin!

What are you doing here? Looking for bargains?

Sh!...Highly confidential!... Special operation: pickpockets.

But that didn't stop us from finding this job-lot of walking sticks.

How much?

Eight bob for the lot.

Six shillings.

Seven...but I'm robbin' meself...

See? You've always got to haggle a bit, here.

?

My wallet's been stolen!

But that's absurd!... You must have left it at home... or perhaps you've lost it?

No, I'm sure someone's stolen it!

Here, you hold these sticks. I'll pay.

Just the sort of thing that would happen to you!... To go and let someone pinch your wallet!

?

Mine's gone too!

Here, let me pay for them.

Thanks very much, Tintin. We'll pay you back tomorrow.

There.

Goodbye! We're going to report this straight away ...

Stop thief!... Help!... My suitcase!...

What's going on?

They caught some thieves red-handed.

Special Branch! Special Branch!... You can tell that to the Inspector!

Snowy!... Snowy!

All right, I'm coming...

I say, Snowy, isn't that a fine ship!

It really is a beauty. I've a good mind to buy it for Captain Haddock.....

How much?

A quid. It's a unique specimen. It's a very old... er... very old type of galliard.

Seventeen and six!

Done! Yours for seventeen and six.

How much is that ship?

Sorry, sir. I just sold it to this young gent.

!

I'll buy it from you.

I'm sorry, sir, but it's not for sale

Look here, young fellow, I'm a collector... How much did you pay? I'll give you double for it!

Thanks, but I'm keeping it.

How much is that ship?

I'm sorry, sir, but this ship is not for sale.

Look, I'll give you a fiver for it!

A tenner!

NO!

Twenty!

Thirty!

Look here: I want to give this ship to a friend of mine. I'm not selling it, so please don't pes- ter me any more!

Now why were they both so keen to buy my ship?

A few minutes later...

It really is superb... Captain Haddock will be delighted.

RRRING

I expect that's him...

I apologise : it's me again!

?

Forgive me if I am too insistent. But as I explained, I'm a col-lector - a collector of model ships. And I would be so very grateful if you would agree to sell me your ship.

I've already told you, I bought it for a friend...

Exactly! Now I have other ships just as good as yours, and we could exchange them so that your friend...

It's no good. Please don't go on. I'm keeping it.

Very well. But think it over. I'll give you my card, so that if you change your mind ...

I shouldn't count on it!

Well, I shall hope.

Goodbye, sir.

CRASH

?

What's happened?

Snowy!... What have you done?

Look, now it's broken!

Luckily it's not too bad. I can soon mend it.

RRRRING

This time it must be the Captain.

Hello!

Hello, Captain. Just the person I wanted to see.

Come on in. I've got a surprise for you.

Tintin, what a magnificent ship!

Thundering typhoons!

Where... where did you find this ship?

In the Old Street Market... Why?

Ten thousand thundering typhoons!... What a remarkable coincidence!... Imagine!...

No! Come with me: then you'll see!

Remarkable!... It's really remarkable!

Here we are! Now...

You'll see...

Look!

Is... is that you?...

No, it's one of my ancestors, Sir Francis Haddock. He lived in the reign of Charles the Second.

But just take a closer look at that ship in the background...

It's just like the one you saw in my room, isn't it?

Exactly!... It's the same ship!... It's identical!... Don't you think that's remarkable?

There's a name here. Look there, in tiny letters: UNICORN

So there is: UNICORN. I'd never noticed it.

Maybe there's a name on mine too... We should have brought it along. Wait here: I'll go and fetch it.

If mine has the same name, that'll really be funny...

Let's see...

Great snakes!... It's gone!

Two days at sea, a good stiff breeze, and the UNICORN is reaching on the starboard tack. Suddenly there's a hail aloft...

Sail on the port bow!

Thundering typhoons!.. She's mighty close-hauled! Ration my rum if she's not going to cut across our bows!

And she's making a spanking pace! Oho! she's running up her colours.. Now we'll see...

!

The Jolly Roger! Pirates!...

Ahoy there!... Clear the decks for action!... Man the poop!... Stand by to haul the wind!

Turning on to the wind with all sails set, risking her masts, the UNICORN tries to outsail the dreaded Barbary buccaneers...

Thundering typhoons! It's no use... She's overhauling us fast!

They must outwit the pirates. The Captain makes a daring plan. He'll wear ship, then pay off on the port tack. As the UNICORN comes abreast of the pirate he'll loose off a broadside... No sooner said than done!...

Ready about!... Let go braces!... Beat gunners to quarters!

The UNICORN has gybed completely round. Taken by surprise, the pirates have no time to alter course. The royal ship bears down upon them... Steady...

FIRE!

Got her!

Got her, yes! But not a crippling blow. The pirate ship in turn goes about - and look! she's hoisted fresh colours to the mast-head!

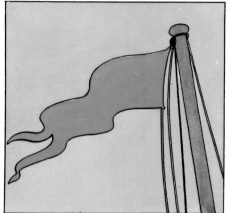

The red pennant!... No quarter given!... A fight to the death, no prisoners taken! You understand? If we're beaten, then it's every man to Davy Jones's locker!

The pirates take up the chase - they draw closer... and closer... Throats are dry aboard the UNICORN.

Close hauled, the enemy falls in line astern with UNICORN, avoiding the fire of her guns ... She draws closer...

Then suddenly, not more than half a cable's length away, she slips from under the UNICORN's poop...whoosh, like that!

Then she resumes her course. The two ships are now alongside. The boarders prepare for action ...

Here they come! Grappling irons are hurled from the enemy ship. With hideous yells the pirates stream aboard the UNICORN.

All hands to repel boarders!

Whew! I just saved it in time!

BOOM

This time it's Tintin... We've got him now.

He can't be far off...

There he is!... Stop!... Stop!... or I'll shoot!

BANG BANG

A counting-frame!... that gives me an idea...

CRACK

Now I see what he meant - the man who was shot - pointing to the birds. He was giving us the name of his attackers! ... Just look at this letter ...

Messrs. M. + G. Bird,
Antique Dealers,
Marlinspike Hall,
Marlinshire,
ENGLAND.

Quick, let's ring up the Captain ...

Hello ... yes ... it's me ... yes ... Who's speaking? What? Tintin! ... I ... Where are you? Hello? ... Hello? ... Hello? ... Hello? ... Are you there? ...

What am I doing here? ... I ... er ... I'm Mr. Bird's new secretary. Didn't you know that? ...

I ... no, I hadn't heard. Please excuse me, sir.

Hello, Nestor! ... Nestor! ...

Hello, Nestor! ... A young ruffian's broken into the house! Stop him telephoning his accomplices! We're coming at once. Don't let him get away, whatever you do!

Hello, Captain! I'm at Marlinspike Hall! ... Bring the police!

Drop that telephone, you!

... What? ... No, not in Greece - in Marlinspike Hall!

Starlings bite? ... Hello? ... Hello? ... Starlings bite what? ...

Marlinspike, Captain! Marlinspike Hall!

What? ... Martin's bike? ... Hello? ... Hello? ... Thundering typhoons! What's going on?

Marlinspike Hall!... Marlin-spike!

Hello, Captain? Can you hear me?... I'm at Marlinspike Hall! No, Marlinspike's the name!

What?... What sort of game?... Hello! He's rung off!

HELP! HELP!

That was Nestor's voice!

That's torn it! The telephone's broken!

There's only one thing to do - run for it - double quick!

If he's here he can't escape us...

That's one for you, sycophant!

That thug had come round - he was just going shoot you...

Let me go!... I keep telling you - it's all a mistake: I'm not the one to arrest...

Ah, here come Thomson and Thompson... Hello.

It's this little ruffian, this little wretch who broke into the house and terrorized my masters; he's a real gangster, Mr. Detective...

It's true, Nestor acted in good faith. I heard his master say I was a criminal. Nestor believed it.

Then your masters are the criminals. Look what's left of my bottle of three-star brandy! It's all their fault!... They're gangsters!... dizzards!. baboons!

And what's more, we have a warrant for their arrest.

My wallet! My wallet! It's incredible!

But your wallet's there...

That's just what's incredible: no one has stolen it!

By the way, what about that pickpocket?... Have you managed to lay hands on him?

Not yet, but it won't be long now. ..

We got his name from the Stellar Cleaners: he's called Aristides Silk. We were just about to pull him in when we were ordered to arrest the Bird brothers, and here we are...

Quiet! Quiet! Listen to me!

Gentlemen, there has been a miscarriage of justice! This man is innocent, as Tintin said. Won't you take off these handcuffs... and let him go and fetch me another bottle of brandy?

There, my man, now you're free. And we'll use these handcuffs for your masters!

We'll follow you, Nestor. Don't forget: it's to be three-star!

Now, Captain, tell me how you came to be here.

Oh, yes... Right. Well...

Just after your telephone call - and I didn't understand a word of that - someone rang up from the hospital...

... where they still had the little-birds-man. After hovering between life and death, he'd just come round and identified his attackers: the Bird brothers, antique dealers of Marlinspike Hall. It was only when I heard that name...

... that I understood what you meant on the telephone. There was no time to lose: I warned the police at once, and we rushed here ...

WHAM *
* OH!
WHAM
OW!

?   ?

We shouldn't have left the police with those two gangsters!...

Look!... one's escaping!... there! He's just turned the corner!

He's the most dangerous of the two: he mustn't get away!

BRRRR
BRRR

A car! That's a car starting up!

Road-hog!... Cyclone!... Bashi-bazouk!... Steamroller!

Too late! He's gone!

We'll take care of the other one later; let's go and help those two!

Wait: I'll give you a hand...

At last!.. Got it!

Now, my friend, I'm waiting for an explanation...

I'm saying nothing!

Perhaps you don't know that your victim recovered yesterday, and divulged your name..

Our victim? I...Barnaby wasn't dead!

Very well: I'd better tell you everything. When we bought this house, two years ago, we found a little model ship in the attic, in very poor condition...

The UNICORN?

Yes, and when we were trying to restore the model we came across the parchment: its message intrigued us. My brother Max soon decided it referred to a treasure. But it spoke of three unicorns; so the first thing was to find the other two... You know we are antique dealers. We set to work...

... We used all our contacts: the people who comb the markets for interesting antiques; the people who hunt through attics; we told them to find the two ships. After some weeks one of our spies, a man called Barnaby, came and said he'd seen a similar ship in the Old Street Market. Unfortunately, this ship had just been sold to a young man; Barnaby tried in vain to buy it from him.

Yes, we know the rest. It was Barnaby whom you ordered to steal my UNICORN. But because the parchment wasn't there, he came back and ransacked the place - again unsuccessfully. And then? ...

Then? Oh well, I'd better tell you the lot...

Barnaby came back empty-handed. Then he suddenly remembered the other man who'd been trying to buy the ship from you.

And next day he visited Mr. Sakharine, chloroformed him, and stole the third parchment...

That's right. But after he'd given it to us, he and Max quarrelled violently about the money we'd agreed he should have. Barnaby demanded more, but Max stuck to the original sum. Finally Barnaby went, furiously angry and saying we'd regret our meanness. When he'd gone, Max got cold feet: supposing the wretch betrayed us? We jumped into the car and trailed him; our fears were justified. We saw him speaking...

... to you. Panicking in case he'd given the whole game away, Max caught up with you in a few seconds, and shot Barnaby as he stepped into your doorway.

I understand so far: but tell me, why did you kidnap me?

We told you: to make you give up the two parchments you had stolen from us a few days after the shooting.

I see. But I couldn't have stolen them as I didn't know you existed! But I wonder... Perhaps it was...

Yes, perhaps it was Mr. Sakharine who took the two scrolls?

Hurrah! That's it!

At last! He's managed to get it off for me...

Come on, Captain, we'd better help this poor chap...

Ready! Steady! He-e-eave!

Whoops!

Captain, as soon as we return we'll see Mr. Sakharine. I'm sure he took the two scrolls...

Yes, we've only got one...

One! Great snakes! we haven't even got that! The Bird brothers took it! But we can get it back!

Give me back the parchment you stole from my room!

Give it back?... That's impossible... Max has it in his pocket!

!

Ring up the police-station at once; give them a description of Max Bird, and his car number - LX 188. Then we'll go straight back to town...

Right!

Next morning...

Now for Mr. Sakharine...

RRRING

Mr. Sakharine? He's gone away, young man. He won't be back for a fortnight.

He would be away! That doesn't make things any easier!

In the meantime I'll go and see the Thomsons. Perhaps they'll be able to tell me if they've found Max Bird...

Good morning. Are you going out?... I just came to ask you...

Sh! Mum's the word! Come with us!

Where are we going?

You'll soon see...

...and a few minutes later...

RAT TAT TAT TAT

58

Mr. Aristides Silk?

Yes...

I arrest you in the name of the law!

Arrest me?...

Yes, you! You are a thief, sir!...

A thief! Aristides Silk, retired civil servant: a thief! It's a mistake, gentlemen, a shocking mistake!

I'm sorry to interrupt you, Mr. Silk, but could you explain the meaning of all this?...

I... er, yes... Well, I... you see, I'm not a thief: certainly not! But I'm a bit of a... kleptomaniac. It's something stronger than I am: I adore wallets. So I... I... just find one from time to time. I put a label on it, with the owner's name ...

... and I add it to my collection ...

I venture to say, gentlemen, that this is a unique collection of its kind. And when I tell you that it only took me three months to assemble you'll agree that it's a remarkable achievement ...

It's amazing! All these wallets in alphabetical order ...

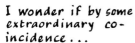

I wonder if by some extraordinary coincidence ...

Hooray!

Property of: Max Bird pinched on 1 - 5 - 58

And here are the two pieces of parchment!... Captain, Red Rackham's treasure is ours!

Goodbye! Don't forget to have a look under the letter T!

Under letter T?

Look under T? Why under T? ...

Good gracious! this belongs to me! ...

"Property of Thompson"! This is yours! ...

Property of Thomson... property of Thompson... Thomson... Thompson ...Thomson...Thompson...Thomson ...Thomson... Thompson... Thompson..

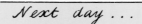

Next day...

Red Rackham's treasure is ours: it's easy enough to say. We've found two of the scrolls, I know, but we still haven't got the third...

It looks as if...

RRRING RRRING RRRING

Hello?... Yes, it's me ... Good morning... What? you've arrested him?...

Not exactly, but thanks to the clues we gave, they managed to catch him trying to leave the country ...

What about the third parchment? ... Did you find it on him?...

Yes, he had it. We're bringing it along to you. But first we've got a little account to settle with this troublesome antique dealer...

Here, Thompson, hold my stick while I just deal with this gentleman...

60

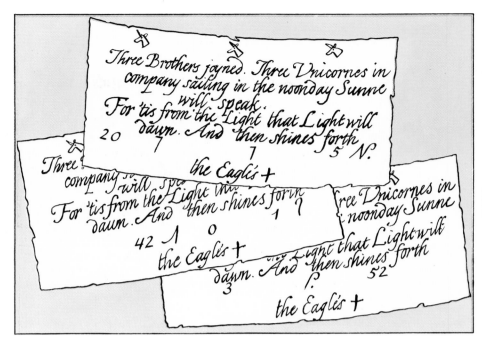

No! No! and No! You can go on hunting if you want to, but I've had enough: I give up. Blistering barnacles to that pirate Red Rackham, and his treasure! I'd sooner do without it; I'm not racking my brains any more trying to make sense out of that gibberish! Thundering typhoons! What a thirst it's given me!

I've got it, Captain!... I've got it!...

The message is right when it says that it is "from the light that light will dawn!" Look, I put them together...

...and hold them, "sailing in company", in front of the light. Look now! See what comes through!...

Thundering typhoons! The numbers and letters are completed, and it gives us ...

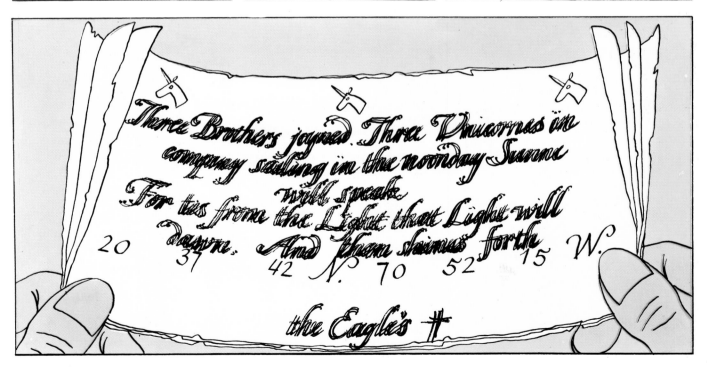

A latitude and a longitude!

Obviously telling us where the UNICORN sank!

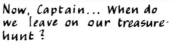

Now, Captain... When do we leave on our treasure-hunt?

When do we leave? ... Er...

Let's see... First we need a ship... We can charter the SIRIUS, a trawler belonging to my friend, Captain Chester... Then we need a crew, some diving suits and all the right equipment for this sort of expedition... That will take us a little time to arrange. We'd better say a month. Yes, in a month we could be ready to leave.

Red Rackham's treasure will be ours!

But of course it won't be easy, and we shall certainly have plenty of adventures on our treasure-hunt... You can read about them in RED RACKHAM'S TREASURE

- HERGÉ -